W9-BMV-587

FOOTBALL'S GREATEST

QUARTERBACKS

Sports Illustrated KIDS

BY MATT DOEDEN

CAPSTONE PRESS
a capstone imprint

Sports Illustrated Kids Football's Greatest are published by Capstone Press,
1710 Roe Crest Drive, North Mankato, Minnesota 56003
www.capstonepub.com

Library of Congress Cataloging-in-Publication Data
Cataloging information on file with the Library of Congress
ISBN 978-1-4914-0758-5 (library binding)

Editorial Credits
Brenda Haugen, editor; Heidi Thompson, designer; Eric Gohl, media researcher;
Gene Bentdahl, production specialist

Photo Credits
Sports Illustrated: Al Tielemans, 4b, 5b, 10b, 14b, 18l, 23, 28bl, 28br, 29t, Bill Frakes, 6b, Bob Rosato, 7,
24t, Damian Strohmeyer, 5t, 21b, David E. Klutho, 12t, 20t, 26l, John Biever, 1, 21t, 22, 25r, 27, John W.
McDonough, 15b, 16t, 16bl, 17b, Peter Read Miller, 6t, 25l, Robert Beck, cover, 10t, 11t, 11b, 16br, 17t, 26r,
28t, 29b, Simon Bruty, 4t, 8l, 8r, 9, 12bl, 12br, 13, 14t, 15t, 18r, 19, 20b, 24b

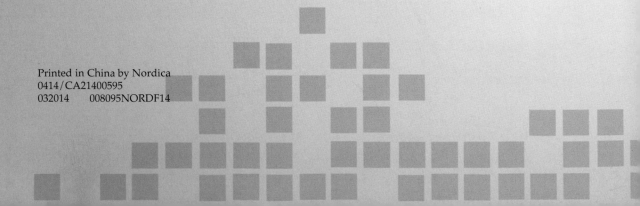

Printed in China by Nordica
0414/CA21400595
032014   008095NORDF14

Table of Contents

*All statistics are through the 2013 season.

TOM BRADY

The score was tied with just over a minute to play in Super Bowl XXXVI. First-year starting quarterback Tom Brady led the New England Patriots onto the field. Brady completed one short pass after the next. Then he hit receiver Troy Brown with a 26-yard strike to put New England in field goal range. Brady and his teammates celebrated their first championship as the ball sailed through the goal posts. Brady was the Super Bowl **MVP**!

It's no wonder many people think Brady is one of the greatest quarterbacks in NFL history. His razor-sharp throws and on-field leadership have helped him win three Super Bowls and make eight **Pro Bowls**.

Few NFL teams wanted Brady after an up-and-down college career at Michigan. The Patriots picked him in the sixth round. He barely played as a **rookie** in 2001. But in 2002, he stepped up and led the Patriots to a Super Bowl title. Brady's best individual season was 2007. He set an NFL record with 50 touchdown passes—a record that stood until 2013. He was named league MVP in 2007 and again in 2010.

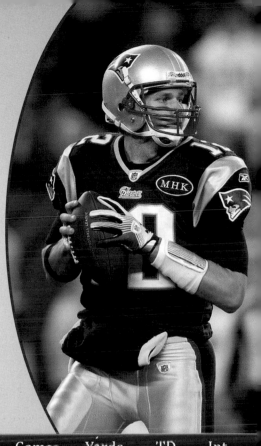

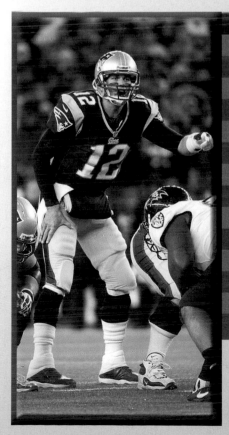

Year	Team	Games	Yards	TD	Int
2000	NE	1	6	0	0
2001	NE	15	2,843	18	12
2002	NE	16	3,764	28	14
2003	NE	16	3,620	23	12
2004	NE	16	3,692	28	14
2005	NE	16	4,110	26	14
2006	NE	16	3,529	24	12
2007	NE	16	4,806	50	8
2008	NE	1	76	0	0
2009	NE	16	4,398	28	13
2010	NE	16	3,900	36	4
2011	NE	16	5,235	39	12
2012	NE	16	4,827	34	8
2013	NE	16	4,343	25	11

MVP—an award that goes to the best player in a game or a season; MVP stands for Most Valuable Player
Pro Bowl—the NFL's All-Star Game
rookie—a first-year player

DREW BREES

The New Orleans Saints trailed the Indianapolis Colts by a point in the fourth quarter of Super Bowl XLIV. Drew Brees and the Saints' offense took over with about 10 minutes to play. Brees was in control. He picked the Colts apart for six straight completions. From the 2-yard line, Brees took the **snap**. He turned and fired a bullet to Jeremy Shockey. The tight end barreled into the end zone for the touchdown. The Saints were in the lead for good.

Brees is the total package. He's smart, **accurate**, and has a strong arm. He's a master at throwing the ball all over the field to a variety of receivers. That makes him a nightmare for opposing defenses.

Brees rewrote the record books in the Big Ten Conference while playing college football for Purdue. But he wasn't picked until the second round of the 2001 NFL **draft**. Some teams thought he was too short. Brees quickly proved them wrong. He played five solid seasons for the San Diego Chargers before signing with the Saints in 2006. As a Saint, Brees became one of the game's best passers. After the 2009 season, he led the Saints to a Super Bowl title. In 2011 he racked up an amazing 5,476 passing yards, which ranks second on the all-time list.

Year	Team	Games	Yards	TD	Int
2001	SD	1	221	1	0
2002	SD	16	3,284	17	16
2003	SD	11	2,108	11	15
2004	SD	15	3,159	27	7
2005	SD	16	3,576	24	15
2006	NO	16	4,418	26	11
2007	NO	16	4,423	28	18
2008	NO	16	5,069	34	17
2009	NO	15	4,388	34	11
2010	NO	16	4,620	33	22
2011	NO	16	5,476	46	14
2012	NO	16	5,177	43	19
2013	NO	16	5,162	39	12

snap—the act of the center putting the football in play from the line of scrimmage

accurate—on target

draft—the system by which NFL teams select new players

ROBERT GRIFFIN III

Ten seconds remained in the first half of a 2012 division game between the Washington Redskins and Dallas Cowboys. Washington's quarterback, Robert Griffin III, rolled to the right to find an open receiver. He fired a pass to Santana Moss in the end zone. Moss grabbed the ball and tapped his feet in bounds. Touchdown! It was Griffin's third touchdown pass of the quarter and helped the Redskins to a big victory.

Year	Team	Games	Yards	TD	Int
2012	WAS	15	3,200	20	5
2013	WAS	13	3,203	16	12

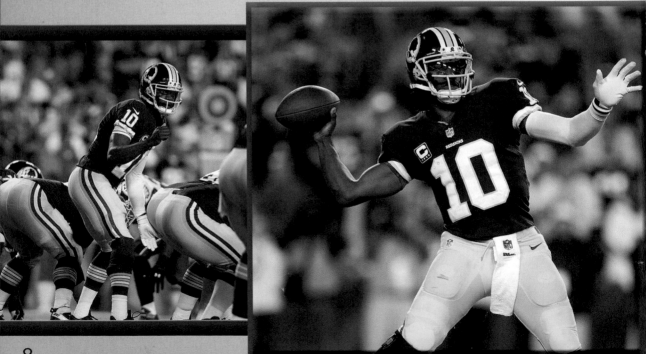

Few quarterbacks are great at both the pass and the run. Griffin, known as RGIII, is an exception. He runs like a running back. But he's just as dangerous when he stays in the **pocket**. His arm strength and accuracy make him a nightmare to defend.

Griffin was a football and track star at Baylor. He won the **Heisman Trophy** in 2011. The Redskins traded for the rights to draft him second overall in 2012. Griffin had a great rookie season. He threw 20 touchdown passes and ran for seven more scores. He was voted Offensive Rookie of the Year. Griffin suffered a terrible knee injury during a playoff game that season. But he returned in 2013 as the opening-day starter for the Redskins. In one of his biggest games of the season, he passed for 298 yards and two touchdowns in a 45-41 win over the Chicago Bears.

pocket—the area behind the offensive line from which a quarterback usually throws passes

Heisman Trophy—an award given to the best college football player each season

COLIN KAEPERNICK

The San Francisco 49ers and Green Bay Packers were tied 24-24 in a 2013 playoff game. 49ers quarterback Colin Kaepernick faked a handoff. Then he darted to his right. He turned on the jets and sliced 56 yards through the defense to the end zone. The amazing running play was a big part of his quarterback-record 181 rushing yards in a playoff game. And it was a key to a thrilling San Francisco 49ers victory.

Year	Team	Games	Yards	TD	Int
2011	SF	3	35	0	0
2012	SF	13	1,814	10	3
2013	SF	16	3,197	21	8

In 2012 people began thinking differently about how quarterbacks could play in the NFL. Kaepernick was one of the biggest reasons. He is a pure athlete. He's got a rocket for an arm. And he can beat a defense just as easily with his legs.

Kaepernick was a touchdown-making machine at Nevada before entering the 2011 draft. The 49ers picked him in the second round. Kaepernick played little as a rookie, and he started 2012 as a backup. But once he got the starting job, he never looked back. He was great during his seven regular-season starts and even better in the playoffs. Kaepernick used his arm and legs to lead the 49ers all the way to the Super Bowl. Then, in 2013, Kaepernick and the 49ers just missed making it back for a second straight year.

ANDREW LUCK

In just his fourth NFL game, Indianapolis Colts quarterback Andrew Luck trailed the Green Bay Packers by five points. With only 39 seconds remaining, the rookie took the snap at the four-yard line. The Packers' pass rush was coming, but Luck was too quick. He fired a bullet over the middle to receiver Reggie Wayne. Wayne turned and fell over the goal line for a touchdown. Luck and the Colts had done it!

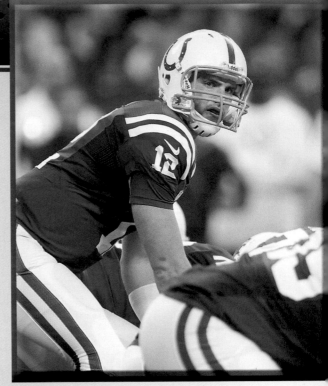

Year	Team	Games	Yards	TD	Int
2012	IND	16	4,374	23	18
2013	IND	16	3,822	23	9

Few young quarterbacks have Luck's ability to see the field and make the right play. He's a good athlete who can run the ball when everything breaks down.

Luck was one of the nation's top college quarterbacks at Stanford. His all-around passing ability made him one of the hottest college quarterbacks ever to enter the NFL. The Colts made him the Number 1 pick in the 2012 draft. Luck quickly rewarded them. He threw for more than 4,000 yards, led the Colts to the playoffs, and made the Pro Bowl. That's quite a rookie year!

In their first playoff game after the 2013 season, Luck brought the Colts back from a 28-point deficit. The Colts beat Kansas City 45-44, and Luck earned his first playoff win.

ELI MANNING

The New York Giants trailed the
New England Patriots in Super Bowl XLII.
A minute remained on the clock. Giants
quarterback Eli Manning dropped back.
New England defenders swarmed
all around him, but Manning
somehow escaped. He heaved
a pass down the field.
Receiver David Tyree
reached up and
caught the ball,
pinning it to the top
of his helmet. A few
plays later, Manning hit
receiver Plaxico Burress with the game-winning
touchdown pass. The Giants were the champs!

Manning entered the NFL with a lot of expectations. His dad, Archie, and older brother Peyton were both NFL quarterbacks. Manning's natural skills and famous football family helped make him the first pick of the 2004 draft.

Manning struggled early in his career, but he caught fire in the playoffs after the 2007 season. He led the Giants to four straight wins and a Super Bowl title. Then he did it again after the 2010 season. With two Super Bowl MVP trophies, Manning stands as one of the greatest playoff performers in NFL history.

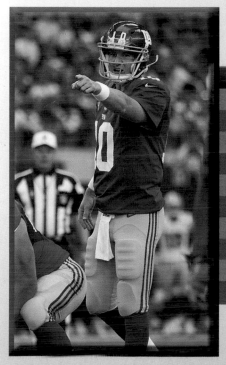

Year	Team	Games	Yards	TD	Int
2004	NYG	9	1,043	6	9
2005	NYG	16	3,762	24	17
2006	NYG	16	3,244	24	18
2007	NYG	16	3,336	23	20
2008	NYG	16	3,238	21	10
2009	NYG	16	4,021	27	14
2010	NYG	16	4,002	31	25
2011	NYG	16	4,933	29	16
2012	NYG	16	3,948	26	15
2013	NYG	16	3,818	18	27

PEYTON MANNING

Peyton Manning and the Denver Broncos were facing Houston in December 2013. Manning already had 50 touchdown passes for the season. One more would give him the NFL record. He took the snap at Houston's 25-yard line as tight end Julius Thomas streaked down the sideline. Manning fired into the end zone. Thomas grabbed the perfect pass. Manning had the new record, and the Broncos got a big victory.

Manning may be the greatest pure passer the game has ever seen. Nobody is better at running a complex offense. Fans love the way he gestures and barks out signals to his teammates before each play.

Manning, the son of NFL quarterback Archie Manning and brother of Eli Manning, was the top pick in the 1998 draft. It didn't take him long to become one of the game's greatest quarterbacks. He won his first league MVP in 2003. Then he did it again in 2004, 2008, 2009, and 2013.

Manning also led the Colts to a Super Bowl title following the 2006 season. He missed all of 2011 with a neck injury. But he returned in 2012 with the Denver Broncos and was the NFL Comeback Player of the Year. Then in 2013, he set a new NFL record with 55 touchdown passes and led his team to the Super Bowl.

Year	Team	Games	Yards	TD	Int
1998	IND	16	3,739	26	28
1999	IND	16	4,135	26	15
2000	IND	16	4,413	33	15
2001	IND	16	4,131	26	23
2002	IND	16	4,200	27	19
2003	IND	16	4,267	29	10
2004	IND	16	4,557	49	10
2005	IND	16	3,747	28	10
2006	IND	16	4,397	31	9
2007	IND	16	4,040	31	14
2008	IND	16	4,002	27	12
2009	IND	16	4,500	33	16
2010	IND	16	4,700	33	17
2011	IND	0	0	0	0
2012	DEN	16	4,659	37	11
2013	DEN	16	5,477	55	10

CAM NEWTON

Carolina quarterback Cam Newton stood in the **shotgun formation** in a 2012 game against Atlanta. He received the snap and faked a handoff. The defense was fooled. Newton darted to his left and streaked down the field. He avoided one last Atlanta defender and did a front flip into the end zone. The crowd went wild! It was a 72-yard rushing touchdown and led to a 30-20 Carolina victory.

Year	Team	Games	Yards	TD	Int
2011	CAR	16	4,051	21	17
2012	CAR	16	3,869	19	12
2013	CAR	16	3,379	24	13

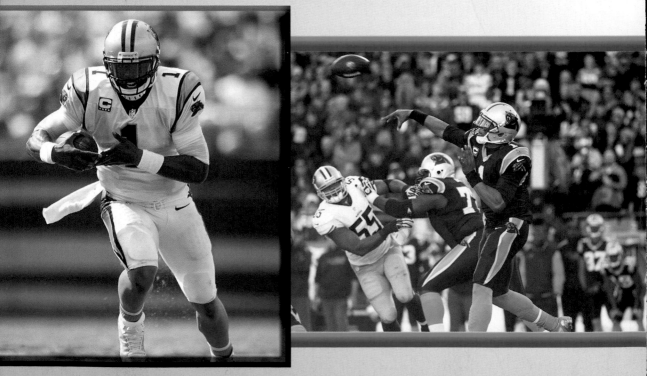

Newton is a true dual threat. He's just as dangerous running the ball as he is throwing it. He's built more like a big, strong tight end than a normal quarterback. His ability to hurt a defense with his arm or his legs makes him one of the most dangerous quarterbacks in the game.

Newton won the Heisman Trophy as college football's best player in 2010. He went on to lead Auburn to the national championship. Carolina grabbed him with the top pick in the 2011 draft. Newton quickly proved himself a great choice. He threw for more than 4,000 yards and ran for more than 700. That earned him the Offensive Rookie of the Year award and a trip to the Pro Bowl. He had his best season yet in 2013 and led the Panthers to the playoffs.

shotgun formation—an offensive formation in which the quarterback begins several yards behind the offensive line

AARON RODGERS

Super Bowl XLV was tied 0-0 in the first quarter. The Green Bay Packers were driving against the Pittsburgh Steelers. Aaron Rodgers dropped back and lofted a pass toward the sideline. Receiver Jordy Nelson caught the ball on the run and tumbled into the end zone. Touchdown! The Packers took the lead and never gave it up.

Year	Team	Games	Yards	TD	Int
2005	GB	3	65	0	1
2006	GB	2	46	0	0
2007	GB	2	218	1	0
2008	GB	16	4,038	28	13
2009	GB	16	4,434	30	7
2010	GB	15	3,922	28	11
2011	GB	15	4,643	45	6
2012	GB	16	4,295	39	8
2013	GB	9	2,536	17	6

Rodgers is one of the most gifted passers in the NFL. His strong arm and accurate delivery make him the complete package. He is among the best at spreading the ball around to many receivers.

Rodgers started just two seasons for California before entering the 2005 NFL draft. The Packers picked him 24th. He started as the backup to Brett Favre but got to start in 2007. Rodgers led the Packers to a Super Bowl title following the 2010 season, and he was named the 2011 league MVP. In 2013 he came back from an injury to help push the Packers into the playoffs for the fifth straight year.

TONY ROMO

Dallas Cowboys quarterback Tony Romo stood several yards behind the line during a 2012 game against the Washington Redskins. The center snapped the ball, and Romo dropped back to scan the field. Redskins defenders crashed into the pocket, so Romo rolled to his right. He spotted receiver Dez Bryant over the middle of the field. On the run, Romo flung a perfect pass that hit Bryant. Nobody could catch the speedy receiver. It was an 85-yard touchdown pass, the longest of Romo's career.

Year	Team	Games	Yards	TD	Int
2006	DAL	10	2,903	19	13
2007	DAL	16	4,211	36	19
2008	DAL	13	3,448	26	14
2009	DAL	16	4,483	26	9
2010	DAL	6	1,605	11	7
2011	DAL	16	4,184	31	10
2012	DAL	16	4,903	28	19
2013	DAL	15	3,828	31	10

In 2002 Romo won the Walter Payton Award while at Eastern Illinois. The award goes to the best college football player in Division 1-AA. But because he was from a small school, nobody picked Romo in the 2003 draft. He ended up signing with the Cowboys, but he didn't throw a single pass during his first three seasons.

Romo finally took over as the Cowboys' starter during the 2006 season. He led the Cowboys to the playoffs and made the Pro Bowl. With his strong, accurate arm and fearless approach, Romo quickly became one of the game's best passers. Opposing defenses know that the three-time Pro Bowl quarterback is a huge threat every time he drops back.

MATT RYAN

The Atlanta Falcons were behind by a point with just 31 seconds to go during the 2012 playoffs. Matt Ryan led his team to the line and took the snap. He dropped back and zipped a 22-yard strike to receiver Harry Douglas. On the next play, Ryan hit tight end Tony Gonzalez with a 19-yard pass. The quick plays led the Falcons to the game-winning field goal and Ryan's first playoff victory.

Year	Team	Games	Yards	TD	Int
2008	ATL	16	3,440	16	11
2009	ATL	14	2,916	22	14
2010	ATL	16	3,705	28	9
2011	ATL	16	4,177	29	12
2012	ATL	16	4,719	32	14
2013	ATL	16	4,515	26	17

"Matty Ice" is known for his calm under pressure. He doesn't have the strongest arm. But he knows how to win when it matters. He led the NFL in game-winning drives in 2010 and again in 2012.

Ryan was a star at Boston College before the Falcons picked him third overall in the 2008 NFL draft. As a rookie, Ryan led the Falcons to the playoffs and was named Offensive Rookie of the Year. Ryan is an accurate passer and led the NFL in completion percentage in 2012. The Falcons have a lot of weapons around him, and Ryan is great at putting the ball where it needs to be.

MATTHEW STAFFORD

The Detroit Lions were struggling. They trailed Dallas by 24 points in a 2011 matchup. Then quarterback Matthew Stafford took control. Stafford whipped the ball all over the field. Slowly the Lions came back. Down by three points in the fourth quarter, Stafford took the snap, dropped back, and spotted receiver Calvin Johnson. Stafford threw a dart into tight **coverage**. Johnson reached up and caught the ball. Touchdown! Stafford had led the Lions to a huge comeback victory!

coverage—the setup of defenders covering receivers and trying to stop them from catching passes

When it comes to pure arm strength, few quarterbacks can match Stafford. With a cannon for an arm, he excels at zipping long passes down the field for big gains.

Stafford starred at the University of Georgia before the Lions made him the Number 1 pick in 2009. Stafford struggled with injuries his first two seasons. But he really showed what he could do in 2011. He became the fourth passer in history to throw for more than 5,000 yards in a single season. He also led the league in passes thrown in 2011 and 2012. The following year, he threw 29 touchdown passes. He even scored a one-yard touchdown in a dramatic win against Dallas.

Year	Team	Games	Yards	TD	Int
2009	DET	10	2,267	13	20
2010	DET	3	535	6	1
2011	DET	16	5,038	41	16
2012	DET	16	4,967	20	17
2013	DET	16	4,650	29	19

RUSSELL WILSON

The Seattle Seahawks trailed the San Francisco 49ers by four points in a playoff game following the 2013 season. A trip to the Super Bowl was on the line. Seattle quarterback Russell Wilson dropped back on fourth down and seven. He spotted Jermaine Kearse sprinting down the middle of the field. Wilson let the ball fly, and Kearse pulled it in for a 35-yard touchdown and a Seattle victory!

Year	Team	Games	Yards	TD	Int
2012	SEA	16	3,118	26	10
2013	SEA	16	3,357	26	9

When it comes to pure athletic ability, few can match Seattle's Russell Wilson. He was a star quarterback in college while also playing second base in the Colorado Rockies' minor league baseball system.

At just 5 feet 11 inches (180 centimeters), Wilson is shorter than most NFL quarterbacks. Many teams overlooked him in the 2012 draft. The Seahawks grabbed him in the third round, and Wilson paid off big. He rushed for four touchdowns his first season and led Seattle to the playoffs, earning him Rookie of the Year honors in 2012. After the 2013 regular season, he took his team to the Super Bowl, where they defeated the Denver Broncos 43-8.

Glossary

accurate—on target

coverage—the setup of defenders covering receivers and trying to stop them from catching passes

draft—the system by which NFL teams select new players

Heisman Trophy—an award given to the best college football player each season

MVP—an award that goes to the best player in a game or a season; MVP stands for Most Valuable Player

pocket—the area behind the offensive line from which a quarterback usually throws passes

Pro Bowl—the NFL's All-Star Game

rookie—a first-year player

shotgun formation—an offensive formation in which the quarterback begins several yards behind the offensive line

snap—the act of the center putting the football in play from the line of scrimmage

Read More

Doeden, Matt. *Football Legends in the Making.* North Mankato, Minn.: Capstone Press, 2014.

Kelley, K.C. *Quarterbacks.* Pleasantville, N.Y.: Gareth Stevens Pub., 2010.

Scheff, Matt. *Tom Brady: Football Superstar.* Mankato, Minn.: Capstone Press, 2012.

Internet Sites

FactHound offers a safe, fun way to find Internet sites related to this book. All of the sites on FactHound have been researched by our staff.

Here's all you do:

Visit *www.facthound.com*

Type in this code: 9781491407585

Check out projects, games and lots more at
www.capstonekids.com